MYGCSEREVISION

And here it is, the Edexcel A-Level Economics practice Paper...

This booklet contains all the Economics questions you could ever wish for to satisfy your needs to study. It comprises of three practice papers each with an in-depth mark scheme, that even a monkey could understand!

Each paper is 100 marks, with realistic exam style questions. You never know, similar questions could come up in your exams and you will be excited!

Make sure to go through the mark scheme in detail to help with your understanding of the question. Keep trying the question over and over if you do not understand it.

Check out @mygcserevision on Instagram for more study tips

Try not to enjoy the questions too much!

© 2020 Jacob Phillips

Printed and produced in the United Kingdom

First printing 2020

ISBN: 9798656102957

www.mygcserevision.com

Contents

> This book is comprised of three **A-Level** Economic practice papers with detailed mark schemes

MYGCSEREVISION

MYGCSEREVISION

Pearson Edexcel

Level 3 GCE

Economics A

Advanced

Paper 1: Markets and Business Behaviour (1)

Time allowed: 2 hours

First name	
Last name	

Centre number						Candidate number					

Instructions

- Use **black** ink or ball-point pen
- There are three sections in this question paper
- Answer **all** questions in section A and section B
- Answer the questions in the spaces provided – *there may be more space than needed*

Information

- The total mark for this paper is 100
- The marks for **each** question are shown in brackets
- Calculators may be used

Advice

- Read each question carefully before you start to answer it
- Check your answers if you have time at the end

SECTION A

Answer ALL questions. Write your answers in the spaces provided

Some questions must be answered with a cross. If you change your mind about an answer, put a line through the box

You are advised to spend 25 minutes on this section

1 In June 2020 AstraZeneca and Gilead Sciences were preparing for a potential 'mega-merger', creating the world's largest pharmaceutical company.

The table below shows the total revenue for the top pharmaceutical companies.

Pharmaceutical company	Total revenue ($bn)
AstraZeneca	23.57
Pfizer	51.75
GlaxoSmithKline	43.54
Johnson & Johnson	42.10
Roche	50.00
Gilead Sciences	22.40
Novartis	47.45
Other	60.72
Total	341.53

(a) With reference to the data provided, calculate the 4-firm concentration ratio to 3 decimal places. You are advised to show your working (2)

QUESTION 1 CONTINUES ON THE NEXT PAGE

(b) State the name of the type of merger between AstraZeneca and Gilead.

(1)

☒ **A** Horizontal integration

☒ **B** Vertical integration

☒ **C** Conglomerate integration

☒ **D** Organic

(c) 'AstraZeneca and Gilead sciences merger would be the biggest in pharma history'

Explain **one** reason why the 'mega-merger' should not happen?

(2)

(Total for Question 1 = 5 marks)

2 The UK is planning on taxing tech titans such as google, Facebook and amazon because they pay little to no tax

The tax will be levied at 2% on revenues from April 2020. This will be known as the 'digital-services tax'

The graph below represents a supply and demand diagram with the effect of tax

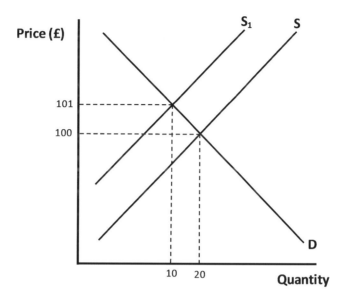

(a) Calculate the total incidence of the tax on consumers. You are advised to show your working

(2)

(b) Suggest the effect of tax on the consumer if PED was 0.2

(2)

(c) Taxation can lead to negative externalities on society. Which of the following is not an advantage of tax. (1)

☒ **A** Distribute income

☒ **B** Shadow economy

☒ **C** Control inflation

☒ **D** Increase purchasing power parity (PPP)

(Total for Question 2 = 5 marks)

3 The following table below shows the long run costs of a clothing company.

Workers	Fixed cost	Variable cost	Total cost	Marginal cost
0	0			
1	300		520	
2	300		680	
3	300	420		
4	300		740	
5	300	480		

(a) Using the table above, fill in the missing gaps for variable cost, total cost and marginal cost. (2)

(b) Using the data from the table, explain the difference between fixed costs and variable costs. (2)

(c) Using the table, at which number of workers does productive efficiency occur. (1)

☒ **A** 2

☒ **B** 3

☒ **C** 4

☒ **D** 5

(Total for Question 3 = 5 marks)

4 eBay has become the world's largest E-commerce platform with a total revenue of 10.75bn in 2019.

Firms on eBay all aim to profit maximise as they all have perfect market knowledge

(a) Using a cost and revenue diagram, show a firm profit maximising on eBay (4)

Cost and revenue | Output

(b) A firm on eBay decides to change their strategy and instead revenue maximise. Which of the following is correct for revenue maximising.

(1)

☒ **A** MR = 0

☒ **B** MC = AC

☒ **C** MR = MC

☒ **D** MR = ATC

(Total for Question 4 = 5 marks)

5 In 2019 a new virus hit all countries causing a global pandemic. Chinese officials promised to make any Chinese vaccine a 'global public good' once available.

(a) With reference to the data provided, suggest **one** problem with making a vaccine a 'global public good'.

(4)

(b) Some people argue that a vaccine should be a merit good in all countries. Which of the following correctly describes a merit good.

(1)

☒ **A** Should not be provided

☒ **B** Encouraged through taxation

☒ **C** Should be provided

☒ **D** Brings less benefit than expected

(Total for Question 5 = 5 marks)

TOTAL FOR SECTION A = 25 MARKS

Question 6 starts on the next page

SECTION B

Read the following extracts before answering Question 6.

You are advised to spend 1 hour on this section.

Extract A

University Finances

For years universities have had a rush to build to attract more students. Universities receive twice as much money per student as they did two decades ago but an increase in spending has meant they are racking up debt. Britain's 130 universities owe £12bn up £5bn since 2012 with 19 universities running deficits. A few are said to be nearly bankrupt.   5

The Tory-Lib Dem coalition suggested tripling student fees to provide income for universities to borrow against. Another less noticed change was to remove limits on the number of students that universities could admit.

Universities such as Leeds, Liverpool and Manchester have all taken advantage of low interest rates by issuing public bonds, raising £250m-£750m each. Less popular unis   10
have looked for private investment and the lowest-ranked unis struggle to find any lenders and are running the biggest deficits.

(Source: Adapted the article 'After the boom, the bust' in the economist)

Extract B

Teach first; Hiring more teachers

Over the past five years the government has failed to meet its teacher recruitment goal by as much as 20% in 2019. The proportion of secondary teachers leaving has increased from 10.8% in 2011 to 11.8% in 2015 and the department of education forecasts on increase in the number of pupils.

Teach first are branching out by offering training for teachers who have quit the   5
profession and those teacher-assistants wanting to be a fully-fledged teacher. Return-ers will be offered flexible working hours. However, teach first is a lot more expensive to train teachers costing £60,000 over 5 years compared to £25,000 taking other paths.

(Source: Adapted the article 'a shortage of teachers prompts hiring' in the economist)

Extract C

Potential for first time buyers

Young Britons believe that the housing market is stacked against them as housing prices have doubled in the past two decades due to tight planning restrictions and low interest rates. The elderly who bought their homes before the boom own a large slice of the overall housing wealth relative to the population and that a 27-year old living today is half as likely to be a homeowner as one living 15 years ago. 5

Yet economists believe that in a decade or two, baby boomers will sell up and downsize allowing the younger generation onto the market. When the boomers begin to sell it would free up the housing market by around 2.5% implying a cut in house prices by around 5%.

Government policy, however, discourages downsizing. Stamp duty makes moving more 10 expensive. The average amount of stamp duty has risen by half in real terms to £8,000. However, council tax has remained the same over 25 years and falls lightly on larger houses.

(Source: Adapted the article 'the silver lining' in the economist)

Figure 1: Housing wealth distribution, January 2017

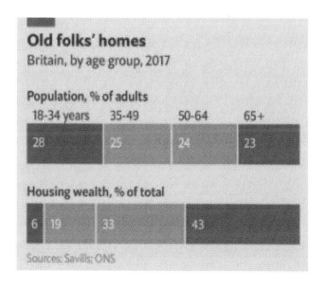

6 **(a)** According to the government, when baby boomers begin to sell it would free up the housing market by around 2.5% implying a cut in house prices by around 5% (Extract C)

Calculate the price elasticity of supply (PES) if there was a cut in house prices by 5% and comment on the elasticity.

(5)

(b) Examine **two** reasons why house prices have doubled in the past two decades.

(8)

(c) With reference to Extract A, discuss the price **and** non-price strategies that universities could use to attract students.

(10)

(d) With reference to Extract B, discuss the likely impacts on teach first in a monopolistic market.

(12)

(e) With reference to the information provided and your own knowledge, discuss the negative externalities associated with a high proportion of the elderly owning large homes.

(15)

(Total for Question 6 = 50 marks)

TOTAL FOR SECTION B = 50 MARKS

SECTION C

Read the following and answer ONE question from this section

You are advised to spend 30 minutes on this section.

EITHER

7   Google is said to be one of the largest monopolies that has engaged in forward and backward integration in order to diversify risk and grow.

Evaluate the extent to which monopolies influence the markets and other firms.

(Total for Question 7 = 25 marks)

OR

8   Evaluate the extent to which small firms can successfully grow using organic and inorganic methods.

(Total for Question 8 = 25 marks)

Indicate which question you wish to answer by marking a cross in the box. If you change your mind, put a line through the box and indicate your new question

Chosen question: **Question 7** ☒ **Question 8** ☒

Write your answer here:

(Total for Section C = 25 marks)

TOTAL FOR PAPER = 100 MARKS

MYGCSEREVISION

Pearson Edexcel

Level 3 GCE

Economics A

Advanced

Paper 1: Markets and Business Behaviour (1)

Official Mark Scheme

Detailed mark scheme to help understand the difficult concepts

Mark Scheme

SECTION A

Questions		Answer	Mark
1	(a)	**Knowledge 1, Application 1** **Knowledge:** 1 mark for the correct formula used • Top 4 firms added together and divided by total. (1) **Application:** 1 mark for applying the formula to obtain the correct answer • 51.75 + 50 + 47.45 + 43.54 = 192.74 • 192.74 / 341.53 x 100 = 56.434281 NB if 56.42 (2dp) given award 2 marks	(2)
	(b)	**Application 1** A	(1)
	(c)	**Knowledge 1, Application 1** **Knowledge:** 1 mark for knowledge of merger • When two companies make a legal agreement to join **Application:** 1 mark for why the merger should not take place • Smaller companies will go out of business/file for bankruptcy • Possible monopoly (if they own 25% share of the market). (1) • Create higher barriers to entry. (1) • Predatory pricing. (1)	(2)
		Total	**5**
2	(a)	**Knowledge 1, Application 1** **Knowledge 1:** 1 mark for calculating the correct area • Area above the equilibrium. (1) **Application:** 1 mark for correct incidence of tax • Price change from 100 to 101 • Quantity change from 20 to 10 • Calculation of 101 x 10 = 1010	(2)

Mark Scheme

Questions		Answer	Mark
	(b)	**Knowledge 1, Application 1**	**(2)**
		Knowledge: 1 mark for definition of a tax or PED	
		• A measure of sensitivity of quantity demanded to a change in the price of a good or service. (1)	
		• A levy imposed on a business or individual. (1)	
		Application: 1 mark for applying the data into context	
		• PED is inelastic. (1)	
		• Consumer will take the burden of tax. (1)	
		• Consumer pays more of the tax / producer will pay less. (1)	
	(c)	**Application 1**	**(1)**
		B	
		Total	**5**
3	**(a)**	**Knowledge 1, Application 1**	**(2)**

Workers	Fixed cost	Variable cost	Total cost	Marginal cost
0	0	0	0	-
1	300	220	520	520
2	300	380	680	160
3	300	420	720	40
4	300	440	740	20
5	300	480	780	40

Questions		Answer	Mark
	(b)	**Knowledge 1, Application 1**	**(2)**
		Knowledge: 1 mark for the definition of fixed cost or variable cost	
		• Fixed cost does not change with output. (1)	
		• Variable cost does change with output. (1)	
		Application: 1 mark for applying the data from the table	
		• Variable cost changes with more output as with 1 workers cost is 220 but with 5 it is 480. (1)	
		• Variable cost is in the short and long run / fixed cost only fixed in the short run. (1)	

Mark Scheme

Questions		Answer	Mark
	(c)	**Application 1**	**(1)**
		C	
		Total	5
4	**(a)**	**Knowledge 2, Application 2**	**(4)**
		Knowledge: 2 marks for a correctly drawn diagram with average revenue and marginal revenue in the correct place	
		Application: 2 marks for the diagram correctly showing profit maximising (MC = MR) 	
	(b)	**Application 1**	**(1)**
		A	
		Total	5
5	**(a)**	**Knowledge 2, Application 2**	**(4)**
		Knowledge: 2 marks for a definition of a public good • Idea that a public good is **non-excludable** and **non-rivalrous** **Application:** 2 marks for identifying the issues with public goods • Idea of the free-rider problem. (1) • Once the good is provided for there is no incentive for people to pay. (1) • Large cost to the Chinese government. (1)	
		Application 1	**(1)**
		C	

Questions		Answer	Mark
6	(a)	**Knowledge 1, Application 1, Analysis 3**	(5)

Knowledge: 1 mark for a definition or formula for price elasticity of supply (PES)
  - A measure of sensitivity of quantity supplied to a change in the price of a good or service. (1)
  - Formula: % change in quantity supplied / % change in price

Application: 1 mark for applying the formula
  - -2.5% / 5 = -0.5. (1)

Analysis: up to 3 marks for linked development;
  - Baby boomers selling will free up larger properties allowing large families to move into bigger houses. (1)
  - Currently 43% of the housing market is owned by people aged 65 and over. (1)
  - A PES of -0.5 means that supply is inelastic. (1)
  - PES is inelastic due to taking a long time to sell houses and waiting for the old to pass away. (1)
  - Houses are not very easily substitutable. (1)
  - Allow the use of a PES diagram. (1)

Mark Scheme

Questions		Answer	Mark
	(b)	**Knowledge 2, Application 2, Analysis 2, Evaluation 2**	
		Knowledge: up to 2 marks for the identification of why house prices have doubled <ul><li>Tighter planning restrictions. (1)</li><li>Lower than expected interest rates. (1)</li></ul> **Application:** up to 2 marks for applying data; <ul><li>Tighter planning restrictions is likely to cause fewer houses to be built and less people to home. (1)</li><li>Low interest rates are likely to increase the number of people wanting to get a loan as it is cheaper. (1)</li></ul> **Analysis:** up to 2 marks for linked development; <ul><li>Less supply for houses will increase the demand (leftwards shift in the supply curve) causing quantity to decrease and house prices to increase depending on the elasticity (inelastic or elastic). (1) – *allow 1 mark for a supply and demand diagram fully labelled*</li><li>Cheaper loans will encourage more consumers to buy houses (idea of a positive wealth effect) increasing the demand (rightwards shift in the demand curve) causing a reduction in supply and an increase in house prices as a result. (1)</li></ul>	**(6)**
		Evaluation: up to 2 marks for 2 detailed points <ul><li>The extent to which house prices have doubled takes along time to occur and the idea that a growing population may influence house prices not tight planning restrictions. (1)</li><li>Magnitude / time lag. (1)</li><li>Some houses have depreciated due to the financial crisis and Coronavirus pandemic. (1)</li></ul>	**(2)**

Mark Scheme

Questions		Answer	Mark
	(c)	**Knowledge 2, Application 2, Analysis 2, Evaluation 4**	
		Knowledge: up to 2 marks for definition of price and non-price strategies • Price strategies: setting the price of a product based on the prices set by competitors. (1) • Non-price strategies: firms seek to increase sales and attract customers through delivery, location, quality and after-sales service. (1) **Application, Analysis:** up to 4 marks for a detailed development linked to the data • Price leadership – certain universities will lead with one price for accommodation / student cost and other universities will follow – this may allow other universities to under-cut competitors. (1) • Price wars – price gets lower and lower for students. (1) • Limit pricing – cutting price to not allow smaller universities to enter the market – lack of **economics of scale.** (1) • Predatory pricing – universities cut prices below AC curve to force out competition in the short term. (1) **Non-price competition:** • Free gifts – universities can hand out free gifts to attract more students. (1) • Advertising – large universities will spend a lot on advertising campaigns. (1) **Evaluation:** up to 4 marks for two evaluative comments • Price wars could cause universities to go bankrupt as they cannot afford to drop the price lower – profit margins fall (shut down point P < AC). (1) • Advertising is a large **sunk cost** and it may not be effective. (1) • Allow reference to game theory (both competitors react and adjust price = lower profits for each). (1)	**(6)**
			(4)

Questions	Answer	Mark
(d)	**Knowledge 2, Application 2, Analysis 4, Evaluation 4**	

Knowledge: up to 2 marks for the definition of a monopolistic competition and a characteristic
- Market that shares some characteristics of a monopoly and perfect competition. (1)
- Characteristic: Low barriers to entry, Profit maximising, product slightly different. (1)

Application, Analysis: up to 6 marks for a detailed and linked answer to the data
- Low barriers to entry – this will only allow firms to make supernormal profit in the short term (other firm can easily take a chunk of the market share). (1) in the long run new companies can enter the market and aim to profit maximise. (1)
- Imperfect market knowledge – firms will not know rivals' price and output decisions (idea of strain on teach first). (1) however supernormal profits can be recognised. (1)
- Recruitment goal failed by 20% - indication for room for improvement attracting more businesses into the market. (1)

(8)

Evaluation: up to 4 marks for two evaluative comments
- Time lag / Magnitude – it takes a long time for a business to set up. (1) and gain economies of scale before they begin to take market share. (1)
- Teach first on average costs £60,000 over 5 years compared to £25,000 over other paths. (1) this could cause a loss of customers for teach first. (1)

(4)

Questions	Answer	Mark
(e)	**Knowledge 3, Application 3, Analysis 3, Evaluation 6**	

Knowledge: up to 3 marks for the definition of negative externalities
- A cost associated with an individual's production or other economics activities, which is borne from a third party. (1)
- Not reflected in market prices. (1)
- Identify relevant negative externalities associated with elderly owning homes. (1)

Application, Analysis: up to 6 marks for a detailed and linked analysis to the data
- 43% of the housing wealth is owned by people aged 65+ with only 6% owned by 18-34-year olds. (1) with 27-year olds half as likely to be a homeowner as one living 15 years ago. (1)
- A high proportion of elderly owning homes means there is less supply for younger generation to buy thus pushing up prices (increased inflation / allow a supply and demand diagram). (1) – this can have a negative wealth effect. (1)
- Homes are not being used to their full potential (inefficiency) (1) as an elderly couple could be living in a 4/5 bed house. (1)
- Allow 4 marks for a negative consumption externality

Evaluation: up to 6 marks for 3 evaluative comments
- Time lag – it takes a long time to sell houses and for the elderly to pass away. (1)
- Magnitude – there would need to be a lot of homes sold to make a difference. (1) stamp duty poses a deterrent for moving homes. (1) the government is against the elderly downsizing. (1)

(9)

(6)

Mark Scheme

SECTION C

Questions		Answer	Mark
7		**Knowledge 4, Application 4, Analysis 8, Evaluation 9**	

Knowledge: up to 4 marks for the definition of a monopoly (allow pure, legal and natural)
- A form of market structure in which there is only one seller of a good or service. (1)
- Identification of the characteristics of a monopoly, e.g. high barriers to entry. (1)
- Explain the role of a monopoly in the market and how it influences other firms. (1)

Application, Analysis: up to 12 marks for a detailed and developed answer
Benefits of monopolies;
- They provide taxation for the government in the form of corporation tax on profits. (1) which can improve the balance of payments and keep local employment high (redistribute income). (1)
- monopolies offer better job security. (1) higher profits for the firm might mean higher bonuses and perks for workers. (1)
- They offer a secure outlet for suppliers (economies of scale). (1) and provide high quality products. (1)
- Monopolies can invest in very expensive high-risk research and development – to improve the quality. (1) and more innovation as they are more likely to take risk without fear of losing market share. (1)

(16)

Mark Scheme

Questions		Answer	Mark
		Evaluation: up to 9 marks for 4 evaluative comments **Costs of monopolies:** • Less choice for consumers and higher prices. (1) potentially lower quality as they have no competition therefore no incentive to make the products better. (1) • Monopolies can easily avoid paying taxes therefore income cannot be redistributed and less expenditure on public goods. (1) • Firms buying from monopolies can be exploited with their terms of trade dictated to them. (1) • Smaller firms may be forced out of the market. (1)	**(9)**
8		**Knowledge 4, Application 4, Analysis 8, Evaluation 9** **Knowledge:** up to 4 marks for the definition of organic and inorganic growth • Organic growth: increasing the scale of operations and gaining market share. (1) • Inorganic growth: taking over or merging with a different company. (1) • Identification of organic and inorganic methods of growing a firm **Application, Analysis:** up to 12 marks for a detailed and developed answer **Inorganic methods;** • Horizontal / vertical integration – small firms can merge in the same stage of production / different stage of production. (1) often to achieve economies of scale or to increase market share. (1) e.g. get access to patients and IPs • Conglomerate integration / diversification – small firms can merge with an unrelated business. (1) to diversify risk and to allow cross-subsidies to help a start up business. (1) e.g. Richard Branson's Virgin Group **Organic methods:** • advertising in order to attract new customers. (1)	

Questions		Answer	Mark
		• Reinvest profits into sunk costs. (1) • Invest in a website. (1) • Attend conferences. (1)	(16)
		Evaluation: up to 9 marks for 4 evaluation comments • Magnitude – larger firms may not want to merger with a small firm as they do not seem 'worthy'. (1) and there may be conflict with the board of directors. (1) • Time lag – merging can take a long time and become very costly potentially losing market share before the merger has begun. (1) • Small firms may have a lack of economics of scale and organic growth cannot fix this without more labour. (1) • Organic growth can be time consuming and is very high in sunk costs e.g. advertising. (1) • Lack of motivation – the business may be satisficing / risk adverse or a hobby. (1)	(9)

MYGCSEREVISION

Pearson Edexcel

Level 3 GCE

Economics A

Advanced

Paper 1: Markets and Business Behaviour (2)

Time allowed: 2 hours

First name	
Last name	

| Centre number | | | | | | Candidate number | | | | | |

Instructions

- Use **black** ink or ball-point pen
- There are three sections in this question paper
- Answer **all** questions in section A and section B
- Answer the questions in the spaces provided – *there may be more space than needed*

Information

- The total mark for this paper is 100
- The marks for **each** question are shown in brackets
- Calculators may be used

Advice

- Read each question carefully before you start to answer it
- Check your answers if you have time at the end

Answer ALL questions. Write your answers in the spaces provided

Some questions must be answered with a cross. If you change your mind about an answer, put a line through the box

You are advised to spend 25 minutes on this section

1 Below shows a cost and revenue diagram of a firm profit maximising in the short run. It shows marginal cost, marginal revenue, average cost and average revenue.

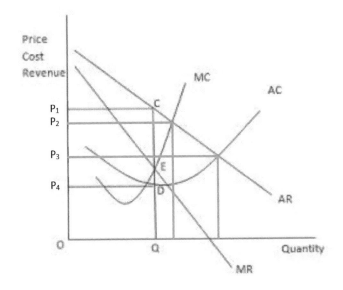

(a) Which price on the cost and revenue diagram represents **welfare maximisation**.

(1)

    ☒ **A** P_1

    ☒ **B** P_2

    ☒ **C** P_3

    ☒ **D** P_4

(b) Under Monopolistic competition firms aim to profit maximise. Explain **one** characteristic of monopolistic competition.

(2)

(c) With reference to the cost and revenue diagram, explain the difference between normal profit and supernormal profit.

(2)

(Total for Question 1 = 5 marks)

2   The diagram below shows a production possibility frontier (PPF) for consumer goods and capital goods.

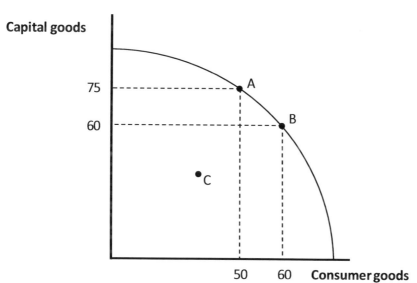

(a) Using the production possibility frontier, calculate the opportunity cost of producing more consumer goods

(2)

(b) With reference to the production possibility frontier (PPF), explain the law of increasing opportunity cost.

(2)

(c) On the production possibility frontier, what does point C illustrate.

(1)

☒ **A** Productive efficiency

☒ **B** Allocative efficiency

☒ **C** Unemployment

☒ **D** X – Inefficiency

(Total for Question 2 = 5 marks)

Turn over for question 3

3 In April 2020 the national living and minimum wage was increased for over 25 year olds by 6.2% from £8.21 to £8.72. This pay rise was aimed to benefit over 2.8 million people in the UK.

(a) Use the supply and demand diagram to show the effect of an increase in the national minimum wage.

(2)

(b) Suggest and explain **one** disadvantage of a rise in the National minimum wage.

(2)

(c) Which of the following is incorrect about minimum price schemes.

(1)

☒ **A** Attempt at price stability

☒ **B** Does not guarantee prices

☒ **C** Costly to taxpayers

☒ **D** Reduces price fluctuations

(Total for Question 3 = 5 marks)

4 A firm recognises a niche in the market and begins to exploit it by making new, innovative products. However, this firm notices another company competing against them in the same niche market.

(a) Suggest and explain **two** ways the firm can become more efficient and outperform its competitor.

(4)

(b) At which point on a cost and revenue diagram can a firm be said to make supernormal profits.

(1)

☒ **A** $MC < AC$

☒ **B** $TC > TR$

☒ **C** $AC > MC$

☒ **D** $TR > TC$

(Total for Question 4 = 5 marks)

Turn over for question 5

5 In 2008 the economy went into a recession due to the housing market crash
known as the financial crisis. In order to stimulate the economy large fiscal policies
and competition between firms was increased.

(a) Explain **two** macroeconomic measures to help enhance competition.

(4)

(b) Regulation methods are often used to stop large firms abusing powers such as
legal monopolies.

Which of the following regulation methods would be beneficial for a firm
wanting to scale up their office facilities.

(1)

☒ **A** Performance targets

☒ **B** RPI - X

☒ **C** RPI + K

☒ **D** Rate of return regulation

(Total for Question 5 = 5 marks)

TOTAL FOR SECTION A = 25 MARKS

SECTION B

Read the following extracts before answering Question 6.

You are advised to spend 1 hour on this section.

Extract A

CMA raises fintech merger concerns

FNZ and GBST are both retail investment platforms in the UK. FNZ acquired financial company GBST in November 2019 in a deal which valued the firm at £152m. However, the Competition and Markets Authority (CMA) said it was concerned that the merger could result in UK investors losing out as a result of higher prices, fewer options and less innovation.   5

In the investigation by the CMA they had found that FNZ and GBST were close competitors in a concentrated market with few significant suppliers. As a results smaller or less well-established firms might find it difficult to enter or scale up because of the risks and reluctance of customers to change suppliers. They found that FNZ is already the largest supplier and is wanting to merge with an established rival.   10

(Source: Adapted the article 'competition watchdog raises fintech merger concerns' in the BBC)

Extract B

$22bn hit for Shell

Shell, the largest oil company in the world is expected to take a hit of $22bn due to a fall in oil prices. Countries across the globe have ordered people to stay indoors and not travel as a result of the coronavirus pandemic. As a result, the cost of oil fell to less than $20 a barrel, just shy of a third of the $66 it cost at the start of the year.

Oil companies such as Shell and BP are trying to reform themselves, dabbling into   5
greener energy as there is no guarantee the transport sector will fully recover as after the pandemic we might have a different attitude to international air travel or physically going into work.

In April 2020 Shell made the decision to cut their dividend for the first time since world war two saving the company millions. However, this is a huge challenge, especially if   10
demand and prices fail to recover.

(Source: Adapted the article 'shell takes hit over lower oil prices' in the BBC)

Figure 1: Brent Crude Price per barrel. June 2020

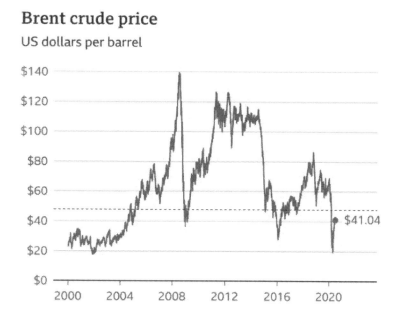

Brent crude price
US dollars per barrel

Extract C

Big rail projects in trouble

Cost overruns on megaprojects are common, with around 98% of construction projects worth over £1bn, are late or over budget. Usually they are 2 years late. And over budget by 80%. Worries about the soaring costs of HS2 have been growing and HS2 is currently one year late. HS2's original budget of £14.8bn has risen 7% to £15.8bn.

Evidence that HS2 is struggling to control costs is building up. Two former HS2 executives were fired after trying to highlight that land purchases for the railway could exceed the budget by billions of pounds.

If costs keep surging HS2 could be cancelled and the funding diverted to areas such as health care and education. However, the biggest problem could be Britain's reputation which could sap public support for future infrastructure spending.

(Source: Adapted the article 'Going off track' in the Economist)

6 **(a)** With reference to Extract B and your own knowledge, explain the impact on the price and demand of oil during the coronavirus pandemic. Use a supply and demand diagram in your answer.

(5)

(b) With reference to Extract A, examine **two** factors that are likely to prevent the merger between FNZ and GBST.

(8)

(c) With reference to Extract C, assess the likely microeconomic effects of the construction of HS2.

(10)

(d) With reference to Extract A, if the merger between FNZ and GBST were to go ahead, discuss the likely regulation methods to stop the abuse of power.

(12)

(e) With reference to the data provided and your knowledge of economics, discuss the significance of the Coronavirus pandemic on firms.

(15)

(Total for Question 6 = 50 marks)

TOTAL FOR SECTION B = 50 MARKS

SECTION C

Read the following and answer ONE question from this section

You are advised to spend 30 minutes on this section.

EITHER

7   Firms on eBay have very low barriers to entry, making it easy for producers to enter and leave the market. As a result, in perfectly competitive markets it is difficult to maintain supernormal profits.

Evaluate the extent to which perfect competition leads to shutdown point in the long run.

(Total for Question 7 = 25 marks)

OR

8   Evaluate the extent to which oligopolies use strategies to help gain market share and economies of scale

(Total for Question 8 = 25 marks)

Indicate which question you wish to answer by marking a cross in the box. If you change your mind, put a line through the box and indicate your new question

Chosen question: **Question 7**   ☒   **Question 8**   ☒

Write your answer here:

(Total for Section C = 25 marks)

TOTAL FOR PAPER = 100 MARKS

Pearson Edexcel

Level 3 GCE

Economics A

Advanced

Paper 1: Markets and Business Behaviour (2)

Official Mark Scheme

Detailed mark scheme to help understand the difficult concepts

Mark Scheme

SECTION A

Questions		Answer	Mark
1	(a)	**Application 1** B	**(1)**
	(b)	**Knowledge 1, Application 1** **Knowledge:** 1 mark for the correct definition of monopolistic competition <ul><li>A market that shares some characteristics of monopolies and some of perfect competition. (1)</li></ul> **Application:** 1 mark for the characteristics explained <ul><li>Imperfect market knowledge. (1)</li><li>Low barriers to entry. (1)</li><li>Similar goods or services / very little difference in products. (1)</li><li>Firms can set the price to an extent. (1)</li></ul>	**(2)**
	(c)	**Knowledge 1, Application 1** **Knowledge:** 1 mark for the correct definition of supernormal and normal profits <ul><li>Normal profits – minimum necessary to keep the risk-taking resources in their current use. (1)</li><li>Supernormal profits – profits above the minimum required to stay in business. (1)</li></ul> **Application:** 1 mark for stating the difference on a cost and revenue diagram <ul><li>Normal profits – AC = AR / TC = TR. (1)</li><li>Supernormal profits – TR > TC. (1)</li></ul>	**(2)**
		Total	5

Mark Scheme

Questions		Answer	Mark
2	(a)	**Knowledge 1, Application 1** **Knowledge:** 1 mark for understanding opportunity cost • Foregoing the next best alternative. (1) **Application:** 1 mark for correctly identifying the opportunity cost • 10 more consumer goods, 15 less capital goods • Opportunity cost = 15. (1)	(2)
	(b)	**Knowledge 1, Application 1** **Knowledge:** 1 mark for the definition of opportunity cost • Foregoing the next best alternative for another **Application:** 1 mark for applying the PPF with an explanation • Concave PPF. (1) • The more production of consumer goods means more capital goods given up / vice versa. (1)	(2)
	(c)	**Application 1** C	(1)
		Total	5
3	(a)	**Knowledge 1, Application 1** **Knowledge / Application:** up to 2 marks for a correctly drawn minimum price diagram with minimum wage above the market equilibrium 	(2)

Mark Scheme

Questions		Answer	Mark
	(b)	**Knowledge 1, Application 1**	**(2)**
		Knowledge: 1 mark for the definition of national minimum wage • An hourly rate a firm must pay and not pay anything lower to the employee **Application:** 1 mark for explaining one disadvantage • Increased unemployment – firms may find it too expensive to employ labour (depends on elasticity and substitutability). (1) • Increased inflation – workers will want to maintain wage differentials. (1) • Ineffective at reducing poverty. (1) • Increased bureaucracy – legal fees to meet legal requirements. (1)	
	(c)	**Application 1** B	**(1)**
		Total	**5**
4	**(a)**	**Knowledge 2, Application 2**	**(4)**
		Knowledge: up to 2 marks for stating **two** types of efficiency • Productive efficiency. (1) • Allocative efficiency. (1) • Dynamic efficiency. (1) • X – efficiency. (1) **Application:** up to 2 marks for applying efficiency to the question • Productive efficiency – lowest cost per output / constant returns to scale. (1) • Allocative efficiency – welfare maximising / P = MC. (1) • Dynamic efficiency – increase spending on R&D. (1) • X – efficiency – lower costs / produce on ATC curve. (1)	
	(b)	**Application 1** D	**(1)**
		Total	**5**

Questions		Answer	Mark
5	(a)	**Knowledge 2, Application 2**	(4)
		Knowledge: up to 2 marks for stating **two** types of measures • Legislation. (1) • Privatisation. (1) • Deregulation. (1) • Limit mergers. (1) **Application:** up to 2 marks for explaining **two** regulation methods • Legislation – passing laws to force particular behaviour (e.g. selling off assets). (1) • Privatisation – removal of x – inefficiency / removal of government subsidies. (1) • Deregulation – allow more firms to compete in the market / lower barriers to entry / high contestability. (1)	
	(b)	**Application 1** C	(1)
		Total	5

Questions		Answer	Mark
6	(a)	**Knowledge 1, Application 1, Analysis 3**	(5)

Knowledge: 1 mark for stating the impact on price and demand of oil during the coronavirus pandemic
- Demand for oil will **decrease** thus price will also decrease. (1)

Application: 1 mark for applying the data from extract B
- The cost of oil fell to less than $20 a barrel, just shy of a third of the $66 it cost at the start of the year. (1)
- People to stay indoors and not travel as a result of the coronavirus pandemic. (1)

Analysis: up the 3 marks for linked development;
- Less demand as people have been told not to travel therefore less people will be buying fuel for cars / less air travel (contraction in the demand curve). (1)
- Shift in equilibrium and producer surplus decreases. (1)
- Consumer surplus increases due to the lower prices. (1)
- Allow a maximum of 3 marks for the diagram (fully labelled)

Mark Scheme

Questions		Answer	Mark
	(b)	**Knowledge 2, Application 2, Analysis 2, Evaluation 2**	

Knowledge: up to 2 marks for the identification and definition for the type of merger
- Horizontal integration. (1) – merger between two firms in the same stage of production. (1)

Application: up to 2 marks for application (1+1), e.g.
- Competition and Markets Authority (CMA) concerned UK investors could be losing out as a result of higher prices. (1)
- The CMA is worried that there will be fewer options on offer and less innovation. (1)

Analysis: up to 2 marks for linked development (1+1), e.g.
- The merger could cause the two firms to from a legal monopoly (over 25% market share) and set higher prices to maximise profits causing consumers to lose out and pay more. (1)
- Lower quality and less innovation as the firm has no competition therefore no incentive to produce better goods or services. (1) or to offer after-care services. (1)

(6)

Evaluation: up to 2 marks for 2 evaluative comments (1+1), e.g.
- The merger may pay higher levels of corporation tax. (1) which may help improve the countries balance of payments and keep local employment high. (1)
- The merger may allow the firm to invest in more research and development to make products the consumers really want. (1) and the larger firm will create new infrastructure creating jobs. (1)

(2)

Questions	Answer	Mark
(c)	**Knowledge 2, Application 2, Analysis 2, Evaluation 4**	
	Knowledge: up to 2 marks for the definition of microeconomics	
	• The study of economic decisions taken by individual economic agents, including households and firms. (1)	
	• Only firms and individuals can have an effect. (1)	
	Application, Analysis: up to 4 marks for application and linked development	
	• Worsening balance of payments / government deficit. (1) - HS2's budget has already risen by 7% from £14.8bn to £15.8bn. (1) which could result in higher taxes paid by consumers or less provision of public goods and merit goods. (1)	
	• Britain's reputation is at stake since there will be a loss of consumer confidence as HS2 is already one year late and is set for further delays. (1) therefore, sapping public support for future infrastructure spending. (1)	
	• HS2 spending may have a greater opportunity cost in health care and education. (1) as the railway could still exceed the budget by 'billions of pounds'. (1)	(6)
	Evaluation: up to 4 marks for 2 evaluative comments	
	• HS2 will provide a high-speed railway line into London which will help benefit businesses as more people can travel to work. (1) HS2 is also creating employment opportunities both on the job and when the railway is finished. (1)	
	• Magnitude – the extent of the benefit to the travel industry will depend on the capacity of the trains. (1) if there is a large increase in capacity there will be more consumer spending on the trains providing more money in taxation to the government. (1) however, if there is a low capacity it will cause overcrowding and low efficiency. (1)	(4)

Mark Scheme

Questions		Answer	Mark
	(d)	**Knowledge 2, Application 2, Analysis 4, Evaluation 4**	
		Knowledge: up to 2 marks for the definition of regulation and names of the regulation methods • Legal sanctions to prevent the abuse of power (e.g. usually used for utility providers). (1) • Methods – price capping, monitoring prices, performance targets, credit crisis controls, rate of return regulation. (1) **Application, Analysis:** up to 6 marks for detailed and linked development • Price capping – an upper limit on the annual price increase a firm can impose on its customers. (1) RPI – X, where X is the efficiency gains the regulator deems achievable by the firm. (1) RPI + K, where K is the additional capital spending agreed with the regulator. (1) • Monitoring prices – ensuring FNZ and GBST provide price transparency to consumers. (1) to make sure they do not get overcharged (avoid a negative wealth effect). (1) • Performance targets – quality of service of goods or services are checked to reduce customer complaints. (1) penalties applied for missing the target. (1) • Rate of return regulation – fixed profit level based on capital with 'excess' profits taxed at 100%. (1) **Evaluation:** up to 4 marks for 2 evaluative comments • Magnitude – the extent of the benefit to the tech industry will depend on the additional capital spending. (1) if a firm is allowed a large amount of capital spending, regulation will be ineffective. (1) with little capital spending the firm may suffer a loss of customers. (1) • Regulatory capture – the regulator may be too close to the tech industry and be less strict with the rules. (1) subject to soft corruption. (1) • Rate of return regulation – this gives no incentive toward the firm to achieve efficiency savings. (1) causing higher prices. (1)	**(8)** **(4)**

Questions	Answer	Mark
(e)	**Knowledge 3, Application 3, Analysis 3, Evaluation 6** **Knowledge:** up to 3 marks for stating three impacts on firms due to the pandemic • Loss of consumer demand for the goods or services sold by that firm. (1) • Loss of profits / revenue. (1) • Depreciating assets due to the value of the company falling as shareholders lack confidence. (1) **Application, Analysis:** up to 6 marks for a detailed and linked analysis of the data • Demand for the goods or services fall due to consumers staying at home. (1) this will cause a contraction in the demand curve, reducing producer surplus. (1) equilibrium will shift causing prices to fall. (1) consumers will benefit from the lower prices experiencing a positive wealth effect. (1) • Companies will not be generating a profit. (1) therefore, the government will receive less taxation. (1) increasing the budget deficit and worsening of the balance of payments. (1) **Evaluation:** up to 6 marks for three evaluative comments • Magnitude – the length of the lockdown will determine the amount of revenue firms lose. (1) the longer the lockdown the less demand = less revenue. (1) • Time lag – it will take a long time for the government to see an increase in the budget deficit. (1) and for firms to go bankrupt as they may have money in the bank. (1)	**(9)** **(6)**

Questions	Answer	Mark
7	**Knowledge 4, Application 4, Analysis 8, Evaluation 9**	

Knowledge: up to 4 marks for the definition of perfect competition and shut down point in the long run
- A form of market structure that produces allocative and productive efficiency in the long-run equilibrium. (1)
- Shutdown point – if a firm cannot cover its AVC it will shut down straight away. (1)
- Perfect competition has; low barriers to entry, products ae homogeneous, perfect market knowledge. (1)

Application, Analysis: up to 12 marks for a detailed and developed answer
- If a firm is making an economics loss (AC > AR) the firm will withdraw from the market in the long run. (1) reducing supply and increasing prices. (1) a firm needs to cover its AVC with some left over to cover its AFC. (1) the shutdown price is the price below AVC. (1)
- A firm needs to make at least **normal profits** to stay in industry in the long run. (1) In the short run they must let AR = AVC. (1)
- In a perfectly competitive market, there are no price-setting powers. (1) price is set by the market reducing firms profits with only temporary supernormal profits. (1) this can lead to firms making an economic loss to gain market share (AC > AR) shutting down in the long run. (1)
- Firms have perfect market knowledge. (1) therefore, access to technology on which firms are making supernormal profits. (1) due to the low barriers to entry new firms can enter the market taking the profits. (1) creating more competition and an increased chance of shut down. (1)
- Products are homogeneous (identical) therefore firms can only compete on prices. (1)

Mark Scheme

Questions	Answer	Mark
		(16)
	Evaluation: up to 9 marks for evaluative comments • Time lag – the extent to the benefit of supernormal profits will depend on the time of the competitor. (1) if the competitor takes a long time to get established then supernormal profits can be made in the long run. (1) if they are quick then both firms will make normal profits. (1) • Magnitude – the amount of profits will depend upon the number of firms in the industry. (1) if there are more firms then normal profit will be made and at risk of shutdown point. (1) a low number of firms in the industry will mean more supernormal profits. (1) • Shutdown point can be avoided through bank loans. (1) potential mergers. (1) and low AFC and AVC. (1)	**(9)**
8	**Knowledge 4, Application 4, Analysis 8, Evaluation 9** **Knowledge:** up to 4 marks for the definition of an oligopoly including its characteristics • A market with a few sellers, in which each firm must take account of the behaviour and likely behaviour of rival firms in the industry. (1) • Oligopolies have; imperfect knowledge. (1), high barriers to entry (low contestability). (1), have price-setting powers. (1), similar goods or services. (1) • Oligopolies profit maximise. (1) and are interdependent on other firms in the industry. (1) **Application, Analysis:** up to 12 marks for a detailed and developed answer	

Questions		Answer	Mark
		• Price wars – oligopolies will cut prices and the other firm will retaliate. (1) this is to gain extra customers and market share. (1) by increasing demand (allow a supply and demand curve with a leftwards shift in supply). (1) • Predatory pricing – firms cut prices below AC in the short run to force out competition. (1) thus, gaining market share. (1) • Limit pricing – cutting prices the firm charges for the goods or services so new firms cannot enter the market. (1) due to a lack of economics of scale. (1) • Non-price competition – firms can compete on brand image, free gifts and loyalty cards to attract new customers. (1) • Game theory – oligopolies pursue a **maximin strategy**. (1) this maximises the firm's own minimum payoff. (1) • Oligopolies always end up at the **'Nash equilibrium'**. (1) as neither firm has anything to gain by changing its own strategy. (1) **Evaluation:** up to 9 marks for 4 evaluative comments • Overt collusion – oligopolies can openly collude to fix prices. (1) however, this is illegal. (1) Tacit collusion is an unspoken agreement between firms to fix prices or supplies. (1) Collusion is very hard to prove, and oligopolies mostly get away with it. (1) • Time lag – strategies to gain market share and economies of scale can take a long time. (1) as customers may not want to pay lower prices for goods. (1) or not know about the lower prices. (1) since they are loyal to their current supplier. (1) • Magnitude – the extent of the benefit will depend on how much firms decide to cut prices. (1) as a small cut in prices will not persuade customers to change brand. (1)	**(16)** **(9)**

MYGCSEREVISION

Pearson Edexcel

Level 3 GCE

Economics A

Advanced

Paper 1: Markets and Business Behaviour (3)

Time allowed: 2 hours

First name	
Last name	

Centre number						Candidate number					

Instructions

- Use **black** ink or ball-point pen
- There are three sections in this question paper
- Answer **all** questions in section A and section B
- Answer the questions in the spaces provided – *there may be more space than needed*

Information

- The total mark for this paper is 100
- The marks for **each** question are shown in brackets
- Calculators may be used

Advice

- Read each question carefully before you start to answer it
- Check your answers if you have time at the end

Answer ALL questions. Write your answers in the spaces provided

Some questions must be answered with a cross. If you change your mind about an answer, put a line through the box

You are advised to spend 25 minutes on this section

1 The supply and demand diagram below show the different prices for iPhone cables on eBay in a perfectly competitive market.

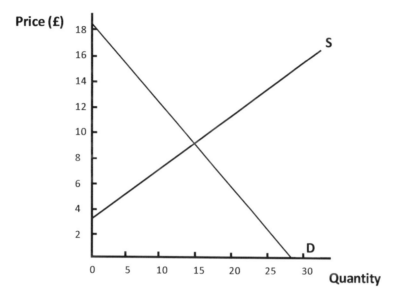

(a) When the market is in equilibrium, calculate the consumer surplus.

(2)

Turn over to continue Question 1

(b) The market equilibrium shifts increasing the total cost to £12 and the quantity to 7 units.
Using the supply and demand diagram, calculate the marginal cost for iPhone cables
(2)

(c) Coronavirus caused a decrease in the consumer demand for iPhone cables, what will be the effect on the producer surplus.

(1)

☒ **A** Decrease

☒ **B** Remains the same

☒ **C** Increase

☒ **D** Goes to zero

(Total for Question 1 = 5 marks)

---

2 A report from Tesco's HQ showed that when Nestle increased their prices of confectionary goods by 6.5%, they noticed a decrease in sales by 11%. As a result losing revenue for Tesco and Nestle.

(a) With reference to the data provided, calculate the price elasticity of demand (PED) for Nestle's confectionary goods. You are advised to show your workings
(2)

(b) With reference to your answer in part **(a)**, which of the following correctly describes Nestle's confectionary goods.

    ⊠ **A**   Unity elastic   (1)

    ⊠ **B**   Relatively elastic

    ⊠ **C**   Perfectly inelastic

    ⊠ **D**   Relatively inelastic

(c) Nestle noticed that when the inflation rate rose above 4.5%, the demand for there cereals increased dramatically.

Explain why the demand for Nestle's cereals increased.

(2)

(Total for Question 2 = 5 marks)

3   Small firms face very high barriers to entry including firms in the technology industry, with an average of 67% of tech firms going bust or bankrupt within the first 6 months.

(a) Suggest and explain **one** legal barrier to entry a tech firm is likely to face.

(2)

(b) Explain **one** barrier to entry that is likely to exist in the oil producing industry. (2)

(c) The strength of the barriers to entry depend upon the market structure. Which market structure is likely to have weak barriers to entry.

(1)

☒ **A** Oligopoly

☒ **B** Perfect competition

☒ **C** Monopoly

☒ **D** Monopolistic competition

(Total for Question 3 = 5 marks)

---

4 Logitech sell between 45,000 – 60,000 products per month. They find that when they sales maximise, the number of products sold doubles per month to between 90,000 – 120,000.

(a) With reference to the data provided, draw a cost and revenue diagram to show Logitech sales maximising.

(4)

Cost and revenue (vertical axis)

Output (horizontal axis)

(b) Sales maximising helps Logitech gain market share and prevent smaller firms gaining economies of scale.

Which of the following is not a reason why firms stay small.

(1)

☒ **A** Price leadership

☒ **B** Limit pricing

☒ **C** Lack of resources

☒ **D** Lack of motivation

(Total for Question 4 = 5 marks)

5   The supply of labour is highly influenced on the demand and wage rate. A study carried out by the UK government, Boris Johnson, showed that the higher the wage rate, the lower the supply of labour.

(a) Suggest and explain **two** labour market failures contributing to a lower supply of labour.

(4)

Turn over to continue Question 5

(b) The demand curve for labour is always downwards sloping. Which of the following affects the demand curve for labour.

(1)

⊠ **A** Skill level

⊠ **B** Trade unions

⊠ **C** Social trends

⊠ **D** Government regulation

(Total for Question 5 = 5 marks)

TOTAL FOR SECTION A = 25 MARKS

Read the following extracts before answering Question 6.

You are advised to spend 1 hour on this section.

Extract A

Bike sales surge through lockdown

During the Coronavirus pandemic Halfords bike sales had risen 57.1% in the 13 weeks up to the 3rd of July as people sought to avoid public transport. The retailer hailed the rise in like-for-like sales of bicycles, but said that at the same time, sales in its more profitable motoring division had fallen 45.4% as the number of car journeys declined sharply.

5

For 2019-20 financial year, Halfords is reporting an underlying pre-tax profit of £55.9m which is down 4.9% on the previous year. However, as lockdown eases Halfords are seeing an increased demand for motoring services again as people begin to use their cars regularly and mandatory MOTs to be reintroduced from August.

(Source: Adapted the article 'bike sales are surging' in the BBC)

Extract B

Britain's high minimum wage

On the 1st of April the minimum wage is set to rise to £8.21 making Britain the worlds highest paid minimum wage and the government thinks it can go higher. However, many economists predict this will cause chaos, as firms will struggle to afford to employ workers leading to a huge jump in unemployment. Yet these fears have not come to pass, unemployment is currently at its lowest at only 3.9%, with employment rate at its highest.

5

Already there are signs that companies in labour-intensive industries, such as hairdressing and hospitality, have responded by raising their prices. Other firms have accepted lower profit margins or have treated their employees as self-employed.

There are better ways of raising the income for Britain's poorest. One would be to boost the provision of targeted in-work benefits such as tax credits (wage top-ups for the low paid).

(Source: Adapted the article 'towards the tipping point' in the economist)

Extract C

Rent controls in London

On January 23rd Sadiq Khan announced that he would develop a blueprint for stabilising or controlling private renters in London. One in four Londoners rent privately, on average sending over 40% of their monthly pre-tax income to landlords.

The mayor does not have the power to control rents, so changes in legislation would be required. However, people are against the rent control as some properties could have their rent fixed in cash, resulting in a real terms fall. Landlords may also skimp on repairs and upgrades. Many may even pull out of the market completely. 5

The labour party is highly against the rent controls too as it would have a large impact on the property market. Landlords would want their tenants to leave. So, may provide a worse service and when possible sell up. A recent study of limits on rent increases and evictions in San Francisco found that policies decreased the supply of rental houses, causing a 5% city-wide rent increase. 10

There are ways to help renters in this situation; building more houses and a cash-term freeze on housing benefit.

(Source: Adapted the article 'Low-rent plan' in the economist)

Figure 1: Average rent increase. January 2015

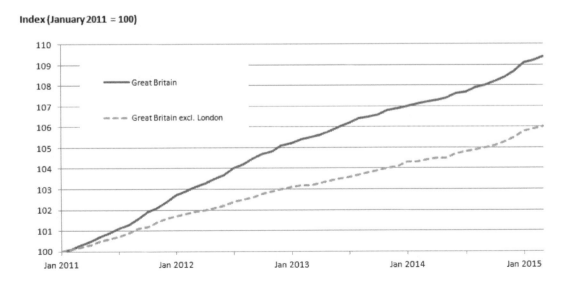

Index (January 2011 = 100)

6   **(a)** With reference to Extract A, explain why Halfords is reporting a decrease in profits of 4.9%. Use a supply and demand diagram in your answer.

(5)

(b) With reference to the data provided, examine **two** possible impacts of an increase in the national minimum wage on the hospitality sector.

(8)

(c) With reference to figure 1, compare the likely factors that may have caused an Increase in average rent prices between the GB and GB excluding London. (10)

(d) With reference to data provided and your own knowledge, assess the likely advantages of easing the lockdown restrictions.

(12)

(e) With reference to the data provided and your knowledge of economics, discuss, using a diagram, how rent control in London may lead to market failure.

(15)

(Total for Question 6 = 50 marks)

TOTAL FOR SECTION B = 50 MARKS

SECTION C

Read the following and answer ONE question from this section

You are advised to spend 30 minutes on this section.

EITHER

7 For years Heathrow airport has been applying for planning permission in order to build a new, third runway. This third runway is needed because of the increased demand for air travel and the increasing population.

Evaluate the likely positive and negative externalities of building a third runway at Heathrow airport.

(Total for Question 7 = 25 marks)

OR

8 Evaluate the different types of economies of scale that firms can benefit from and grow.

(Total for Question 8 = 25 marks)

Indicate which question you wish to answer by marking a cross in the box. If you change your mind, put a line through the box and indicate your new question

Chosen question: **Question 7** ☒   **Question 8** ☒

Write your answer here:

(Total for Section C = 25 marks)

TOTAL FOR PAPER = 100 MARKS

MYGCSEREVISION

Pearson Edexcel
Level 3 GCE

Economics A

Advanced
Paper 1: Markets and Business Behaviour (3)

Official Mark Scheme

Detailed mark scheme to help understand the difficult concepts

Mark Scheme

SECTION A

Questions		Answer	Mark
1	(a)	**Knowledge 1, Application 1** **Knowledge:** 1 mark for the correct values from the market equilibrium • Price: £8. (1) • Quantity: 15 units. (1) **Application:** 1 mark for correctly calculating the consumer surplus • Consumer surplus is the triangle above the demand curve • $(18 - 8) \times 15 / 2$ • Consumer surplus = 75. (1)	(2)
	(b)	**Knowledge 1, Application 1** **Knowledge:** 1 mark for the correct formula of marginal cost (MC) • Marginal cost = change in total cost / change in quantity **Application:** 1 mark for calculating marginal cost (MC) • $(12 - 8) / (15 - 7)$ • Marginal cost = 0.5 or ½. (1)	(2)
	(c)	**Application 1** A	(1)
		Total	5
2	(a)	**Knowledge 1, Application 1** **Knowledge:** 1 mark for the correct definition of price elasticity of demand (PED) • PED: percentage change in quantity / percentage change in price. (1) **Application:** 1 mark for correctly applying the formula • $-11 / 6.5$. (1) • PED = -1.69 (2DP). (1)	(2)

Mark Scheme

Questions		Answer	Mark
	(b)	**Application 1** B	**(1)**

	(c)	**Knowledge 1, Application 1**
		
		Knowledge: 1 mark for the definition of a normal good
		   • Normal good; one where the quantity demanded increases in response to an increase in consumer incomes. (1)
		
		Application: 1 mark for applying the normal good to the question
		   • A rise in inflation rate will cause **real** incomes to rise. (1)
		   • A rise in income will create a positive wealth effect. (1)
		   • When income rises the demand for the good rises. (1)
		   • Allow a mark for an income/quantity graph with a perpendicular line. (1)
			(2)

		Total	5

3	**(a)**	**Knowledge 1, Application 1**
		
		Knowledge: 1 mark for the definition of barriers to entry
		   • Barriers to entry – difficult for new firms to enter the market. (1)
		
		Application: 1 mark for explaining legal barriers to entry firms may face
		   • Patients – license to use the products must be paid. (1)
		   • Government licenses. (1)
		   • Legal barriers to entry make it hard to achieve economics of scale. (1)
			(2)

	(b)	**Knowledge 1, Application 1**
		
		Knowledge: 1 mark for stating the type of barrier to entry
		   • Technical barriers to entry – technological expenses to enter the industry. (1)
		
		Application: 1 mark for explaining technical barriers to entry
		   • Cost of equipment to participate in the sector. (1)
		   • Minimum efficient scales and economies of scale needed. (1)
			(2)

Mark Scheme

Questions		Answer	Mark
	(c)	**Application 1** D	**(1)**
		Total	5
4	**(a)**	**Knowledge 2, Application 2** **Knowledge: :** 2 marks for a correctly drawn diagram with average revenue and marginal revenue in the correct place **Application:** 2 marks for the diagram correctly showing sales maximising (AC = AR) 	**(4)**
	(b)	**Application 1** A	**(1)**
		Total	5

5	**(a)**	**Knowledge 2, Application 2**
		
		Knowledge: up to 2 marks for stating the two types of labour market failure.
		   • Occupational immobility. (1)
		   • Geographical immobility. (1)
		
		Application: up to 2 marks for describing each immobility factor
		   • Workers lack the correct skills for new jobs. (1)
		   • People cannot relocate to another part of the country. (1)
			(4)

Questions		Answer	Mark
	(b)	**Application 1**	**(1)**
		D	
		Total	5

Mark Scheme

SECTION B

Questions		Answer	Mark
6	(a)	**Knowledge 1, Application 1, Analysis 3**	(5)

Knowledge: 1 mark for stating why Halfords has reported a decrease in profits
- Halfords has suffered a decrease in profits due to a decrease in consumer demand for motoring products. (1)

Application: 1 mark for applying the data from extract A
- Halfords more profitable motoring division has suffered a fall in sales by more than 45.4%. (1)
- Bike sales had increased however this is not as profitable as the motoring division. (1)

Analysis: up to 3 marks for a linked development;
- There has been less demand for motoring products since the number of car journeys declined sharply. (1) because the UK was put into lockdown. (1)
- As a result, Halfords suffered a decrease in revenues. (1)
- MOTs have not been mandatory. (1) therefore, consumers have not felt the need to repair their cars. (1)
- Allow a maximum of 3 marks for the diagram (fully labelled)

Questions	Answer	Mark
(b)	**Knowledge 2, Application 2, Analysis 2, Evaluation 2**	

Knowledge: up to 2 marks for the identification of the impacts of an increase in the national minimum wage and definition.
- NMW – a minimum hourly rate that an employer must by law pay all their workers. (1)
- A rise in prices for consumers. (1)
- Firms will begin to make employees redundant. (1)

Application: up to 2 marks for application (1+1), e.g.
- Minimum wage is set to rise to £8.21. (1) however, firms will struggle to afford to employ workers. (1)
- Unemployment is at its lowest of 3.9% meaning there are more employed than ever before. (1)

Analysis: up to 2 marks for linked development (1+1), e.g.
- A rise in prices will cause consumer surplus to decrease. (1) suffering a **negative wealth effect**. (1) therefore, firms will see a decrease in revenues causing more workers to be made redundant. (1)
- A rise in incomes will cause a rise in inflation. (1) and employees will want to keep wage differentials. (1)
- Allow a minimum price diagram with minimum wage above the market equilibrium. (1)

(6)

Evaluation: up to 2 marks for 2 evaluative comments (1+1), e.g.
- Magnitude – the extent of the impact will depend upon the increase in minimum wage. (1) if there is a small increase, there will only be a small rise in prices. (1)
- Time lag – it takes a long time for the NMW to take effect in the economy as it may take months for the inflation rate to rise. (1)

(2)

Mark Scheme

Questions		Answer	Mark
	(c)	**Knowledge 2, Application 2, Analysis 2, Evaluation 4**	

Knowledge: up to 2 marks for stating the trend and defining index numbers.
- London has seen a greater percentage increase in rent prices than the rest of the UK. (1)
- Index numbers show the percentage increase, year on year, allowing comparisons to be made over time. (1)

Application, Analysis: up to 4 marks for application and linked development
- Rent prices have risen because supply is not keeping up with the demand for properties in London (rightwards shift in demand curve). (1) pushing up prices, reducing consumer surplus and increasing producer surplus. (1)
- There is a small number of houses for sale. (1) therefore, consumers only option is to rent. (1)
- House prices are so high that first time buyers cannot afford the homes and are forced to rent instead. (1) they cannot afford the deposit on the house. (1)

(6)

Evaluation: up to 4 marks for 2 evaluative comments
- House prices may be higher in London because there are more job opportunities. (1) and higher paid / ranked jobs with the likes of Canary Wharfs investment banks and hedge funds. (1)
- There are numerous universities in London, therefore the students will take up the cheap accommodation. (1)
- Time lag – the value of properties rises over time; therefore, landlords feel their properties should be renting out for more money. (1)

(4)

Mark Scheme

Questions	Answer	Mark
(d)	**Knowledge 2, Application 2, Analysis 4, Evaluation 4**	

Knowledge: up to 2 marks for stating the advantages of easing lockdown restrictions.
- More consumer spending. (1)
- Higher employment. (1)
- Higher economic growth. (1)

Application, Analysis: up to 6 marks for detailed and linked development.
- Easing of the lockdown will allow consumers to go to restaurants / shops / cinemas. (1) this will increase the amount of money in the economy. (1) allowing firms to make a profit and employ more workers to keep up with the increased demand. (1)
- Fuel stations will begin to make more revenue. (1) as there will be more cars on the road. (1) and a higher demand for oil / fuel. (1)
- Government will receive more money in taxation. (1) as more people begin to go back to work. (1)
- Government budget deficit will improve. (1) as less money is spent on the furlough scheme. (1) and more money can be provided for education and health care. (1) providing more merit and public goods. (1)

(8)

Evaluation: up to 4 marks for 2 evaluative comments.
- Magnitude – the extent of the easing of the lockdown will depend on how much it is eased. (1) if the lockdown is eased slowly with little change the economy will take longer to restart and the budget deficit will worsen. (1)
- Easing the lockdown may mean a spike in the number of coronavirus cases. (1) triggering a second wave potentially causing the lockdown to last even longer. (1)
- Time lag – it will take a long time for the governments budget deficit to improve. (1) as the country needs fiscal and monetary polices to restart the economy. (1)

(4)

Mark Scheme

Questions	Answer	Mark
(e)	**Knowledge 3, Application 3, Analysis 3, Evaluation 6**	

Knowledge: up the 3 marks for the definition of market failure and stating the types.
- A circumstance where the free market does not lead to the optimum allocation of resources. (1)
- Types of market failure; lack of competition. (1), information failure. (1), public and merit goods. (1), factor immobility. (1)

Application, Analysis: up to 6 marks for a detailed and linked analysis of the data
- Lack of competition – imposing rent control will cause landlords to kick out their tenants. (1) and sell the house. (1) because they will not be receiving as much money. (1) therefore, the supply of rental properties will decrease reducing the competition causing the price to rise again .(1)
- Asymmetric information – tenants may be paying their rent in cash. (1) which will result in a real terms fall as there is not as much cash flowing into the bank. (1) and taxation can be avoided reducing the number of public and merit goods. (1)

Evaluation: up to 6 marks for 3 evaluative comments
- Time lag – the extent of the market failure depends on how long it takes to change the legislation. (1) as the major does not have the power to control rents. (1)
- Magnitude – the extent of the market failure will depend upon the amount the prices are changed. (1) if the rent is reduced by a large amount a lot of houses will go up for sale increasing the supply and decreasing prices. (1) if the rent only changes by a small amount there will not be a lack of competition. (1)

Mark: (8) (6)

Mark Scheme

SECTION C

Questions	Answer	Mark
7	**Knowledge 4, Application 4, Analysis 8, Evaluation 9**	

Knowledge: up to 4 marks for the definition of private costs and external costs

- External cost – a cost associated with an individual's production or other economic activities. (1) which is borne by a third party and is not reflected in market prices. (1)
- Private cost – a cost incurred by an individual. (1) as part of its production or other economic activities. (1)
- Externality – a cost or benefit that is external to the market transaction and is thus not reflected in the market prices. (1)

Application, Analysis: up to 12 marks for a detailed and developed answer

- The major private cost of expanding Heathrow are the cost of materials. (1) which will need to be extracted and transported causing congestion on the motorways. (1)
- There will be a high cost of labour as the project could take years to complete. (1) and the cost of the land and planning permission to build the third runway. (1)
- Compensation may have to be paid to residents due to the noise and air pollution. (1) potentially destroying wildlife and reducing the biodiversity. (1)
- There may be a lot of visual pollution created. (1) and an impact on climate change. (1) this will cause stress for residents potentially causing a spike in house sales. (1)
- Allow a negative externality diagram

| | | **(16)** |

Questions		Answer	Mark
		Evaluation: up to 9 marks for 4 evaluative comments • Magnitude – the extent of the external costs will depend upon how big the extension is. (1) if the third runway is very large and requires extra digging and construction there will be more noise pollution and habitats destroyed. (1) if construction does not require much land there will be less biodiversity destroyed. (1) • It is hard to quantify the external costs precisely. (1) • There may be external benefits. (1) as house prices will rise since more people want to use the airport. (1) and a positive impact on UK growth (positive multipliers). (1) • Time lag – construction may take years. (1) and be largely overbudget damaging the government's budget deficit. (1)	**(9)**
8		**Knowledge 4, Application 4, Analysis 8, Evaluation 9** **Knowledge:** up to 4 marks for the definition of economies of scale and an explanation of the long run average cost curve • Economies of scale – the cost advantages that a business can exploit by expanding their scale of production in the long run. (1) • EoS help to reduce the long run average costs of production. (1) • These lower costs are an improvement in **productive efficiency**. (1) giving consumers a lower market price. (1) **Application, Analysis:** up to 12 marks for a detailed and developed answer **Internal economies of scale;** • Technical economies of scale – specialisation of the workforce. (1) will allow products to be made quicker and at a higher quality boosting productivity. (1) • Managerial economies of scale – large scale businesses employ specialists to supervise production. (1) better investment in HR and equipment will also raise productivity. (1) and reduce labour unit costs. (1)	

Questions	Answer	Mark
	• Financial economies of scale – larger firms are said to be more 'credit-worthy' with more access to credit facilities. (1) however, smaller firms face higher interest rates. (1) gaining this type of EoS will help the business borrow more money for capital and buy more high-tech machinery. (1) and become more productively efficient. (1)	
	External economies of scale	
	• Better transportation network will help to reduce unit costs on products. (1) gaining economies of scale (constant returns to scale). (1)	
	• Improvements in research and development. (1) allowing the firm to know exactly what the customer wants. (1)	
		(16)
	Evaluation: up to 9 marks for 4 evaluative comments	
	• Time lag – it takes a long time to achieve economies of scale. (1) as there are larger firms taking the market share and have fixed contracts with suppliers. (1) making it hard to be productively efficient. (1)	
	• Many firms potentially encounter diseconomies of scale. (1) because the firm is slower at responding to change. (1) or has become X – inefficient (no longer operating at minimum cost). (1)	
	• Idea of the principle-agent problem. (1) as the agent may not be focused on achieving economies of scale as their salary is based on revenue maximising. (1) not working in the best interest of the shareholders. (1)	
		(9)

Printed in Great Britain
by Amazon